SCARY, NO SCARY

ALSO BY ZACHARY SCHOMBURG

The Man Suit (2007)

SCARY, NO SCARY
ZACHARY SCHOMBURG

Black Ocean
Boston · New York · Chicago

To reprint, reproduce, or transmit electronically or by recording all or part of this manuscript, beyond brief reviews or educational purposes, please send a written request to the publisher at:

Black Ocean
P.O. Box 52030
Boston, MA 02205

clothbound cover art by Enrique Martínez Celaya:
"Landscape (Breadth)" (2002)
www.martinezcelaya.com

paperback cover design by Denny Schmickle
www.dennyschmickle.com

Library of Congress Cataloging-in-Publication Data

Schomburg, Zachary, 1977–
  Scary, no scary / Zachary Schomburg.
    p. cm.
  ISBN 978-0-9777709-9-1
  I. Title.
  PS3619.C4536S33 2009
  811'.6—dc22

                              2009026214

Printed in Canada

Second Printing, 2011

ACKNOWLEDGMENTS

Thank you to the editors of the journals where these poems were first published: *Absent, Alice Blue Review, Bat City Review, Born, Capgun, Denver Quarterly, Forklift Ohio, Fou, Inknode, Konundrum Engine, Laurel Review, Linebreak, Muthafucka, Phoebe, Pilot, Redivider, Saltgrass, Strange Machine, Third Coast, Typo,* and *We Heart Four Things.*

An earlier version of "The Pond" originally appeared as a chapbook from Greying Ghost Press.

Many thanks to the following people for their help with these poems: Mathias Svalina, Grace Bauer, Jeff Downey, and especially Emily Kendal Frey. Thank you to the editors, Janaka Stucky and Carrie Olivia Adams. And thank you to Megan Durham for telling me the story that inspired this collection's title poem.

CONTENTS

SCARY, NO SCARY

You'll return
to your childhood
home

after a lifetime away
to find it
abandoned. Its

red paint will be
completely weathered.

It will have
a significant westward lean.

There will be
a hole in its roof
that bats fly
out of.

The old man
hunched over
at the front door
will be prepared
to give you a tour,
but first he'll ask
scary, or no scary?

You should say
no scary.

NEW KIND OF NIGHT

There is a new kind of night.
It is never-ending

and nothing can be seen
like when we are in a cave
and I make
inappropriate gestures
toward my sex-parts
while you tell me
you can hear my heart beating,
and about your fear
of being crushed into a tiny cube
from walls moving slowly in.

I can pretend
I am stabbing myself
repeatedly in the chest or
pulling my intestine out
through my navel
and using it
to mummify myself or
pulling my intestine out
through my navel
and tying it
like a lasso to toss
around your torso.

I am a tree
you can't see.

NEW KIND OF TREE

There is a new kind
of tree.

It bleeds.

It grows one meter per minute.

One boy played
too long
in this new kind of tree.
He is too high in the tree
to get down.
His family is busy
blowing kisses.

They look like
tiny insects.

How do you tell someone
their family is
tiny insects?

How do you tell someone
their boy is
a hummingbird?

NEW KIND OF LIGHT

I move my hands
in these woods
to find her sex-parts.

We discover our sex-parts
make heat
and blue light.

We become outlines of ourselves—

long scratches
in the sky.

We have a daughter
who was never born.

She lives in the house
we never built,

but in this new light,
you can almost see
its tattered roof.

YOUR LIMBS WILL BE TORN
OFF IN A FARM ACCIDENT

Your limbs
will be torn off
in a farm accident.

Tree limbs
will grow in those places.

You'll cry at night
as your limbs curl a little around your still-soft face,
as your skin toughens.

A hummingbird will begin
to hover near your ear.

Soon you'll be
more tree
than person.

You'll go camping in the woods
and never come back.

FALLING LIFE

You are in a very high tree.

If you jump
you will live a full life
while falling.

You will get married
to a hummingbird

and raise beautiful part-
hummingbirds.

You will die of cancer
in mid-air.

I will not lie.
It will be painful.

You are a brave little boy
or girl.

THE OLD MAN WHO WATCHES ME SLEEP

The old man who watches me sleep
has wings

growing from his chest.
This is a mistake.

This is why
he's so hunched over.

Sometimes,
his crying wakes me
and I open my eyes a little
to find him
trying to push
those wings
through
to the other side.

If you have a soul
it may have been put in there backward.

THE ABANDONED HOTEL

Inside the woods is an abandoned hotel.
Trees grow in the lobby
and up through the rooms.
Limbs jut out through the windows.
It looks like outside
inside.

I climb the trees
through 1000 rooms.

I look for you
in each of them.

You're a long shiny line.

LOOK THROUGH A COMPLEX EYE
AND SEE 1000 OF EVERYTHING

Look through a complex eye
and see 1000 of everything.

A bird becomes
a black cloud.

A broken mirror becomes
a hotel.

One boy falls from
a tree

and rains on
a cornfield.

Everything I plant
I bury.

THE BLACK HOLE

I found a black hole
behind the abandoned hotel.

When I pushed you into it
you just kept falling
right there
at its infinite lip.

You looked like the second hand
of a clock
without a clock.

You looked like an arm
uncrossing.

OOOOOOOOOO
OOO

That's the sound
you made.

WOMAN TIED TO A TREE

Neither of us have names,
especially you.

I reach out to untie you
but my hands hover

in the space between us
like wolf spiders.

I can't untie you
because you're miles away,

and gigantic,
tied to a gigantic tree

and I'm in your gigantic
upturned palm—

have been
this whole time.

I KNOW A DEAD WOLF WE
CAN CLIMB INSIDE AND BEAT

I know a dead wolf
we can climb inside
and beat

like little hearts.
It would maybe
come back

to life,
the wolf.

It would be feared,
the king of

the forest,
the two-hearted wolf

that rose
from the dead

and we would be
inside it,

our legs
in its legs

our eyes
looking through
its eye-holes,

our bodies
beating, beating.

I FOUND A BEATING HEART
HALF-BURIED IN THE WOODS

I found a beating heart half-buried in the woods. It was beating beneath some dead leaves. When I picked it up, it was warm and heavy in my cold hands. I worried I was going to drop it. Later, I found a woman half-buried not far from where I found the beating heart. *Is this your beating heart?* I asked. She didn't answer. She didn't have a larynx. She didn't even have a thorax. She didn't have anything. Not even arms or legs or a head. She really wasn't a woman as much as she was the space between dead leaves. *No, it's yours* she said.

THIS IS NOT FOG THIS IS COBWEBS

This is not fog
this is cobwebs.

All I have is cobwebs.

I will make a dress
for you

after plucking
with my fingers
from

the fragile silk
a spider

a spider
a spider

O Evelyn,
look

our ribs
are zippers.

I GIVE BIRTH TO A GIRL WHO IS
SO TINY I LOSE HER IMMEDIATELY

I give birth to a girl
who is so tiny
I lose her immediately.

I search for her
in the woods.

I strip the bark
from the trees
until my fingers turn raw.

This is why the trees
are blood-stained
and look like old
gigantic leg bones.

This is why the trees
are blood-stained
and look like soft
jaguars licking
their paws.

I sometimes feel
her moving
in my hair.

A tiny cake is drying
on a tiny table.

I'M RIGHT HERE I'M A KIND OF LAMP

I'm right here.

I'm a kind of
lamp

for you to see
the baby

how you
make

the baby how
you make

the baby
move.

TWO METEORITE THEORIES

If we stand still long enough
a gigantic meteorite
will crash into our skulls and kill us.
Or meteorites crash into our skulls all the time, every day,
but no one notices
because they are so tiny,
constantly crashing,
killing us slowly over decades.
Either way, let's not just stand here
with our fingers up our butts.

I'M SORRY I MISSED
YOUR BIRTHDAY PARTY

I'm sorry I missed your birthday party
I said. *I'm sorry I missed your birthday
party* I said. *I'm sorry I missed
your birthday party* I said. *I'm sorry
I missed your birthday party* I said.
The world. It is a night blooming cereus
opening every once in a while
and closing.

THE SAWING IN HALF

After sawing myself in half
half of me moves to the woods

and buries itself
in a heap of leaves.

The other half of me
builds a house

and moves into the house
and goes to sleep.

Sawing myself in half
is how I make choices.

It is how I avoid
the lava

crawling toward me
as it swallows

some of the trees
and as it sizzles in the river.

a.	*b.*
I am not frightened by Hell.	I'll be unable to survive there without you.

THIS IS WHAT YOU NEED TO KNOW ABOUT THE WORLD, PRETEND SON

When I cupped my hand a broken hummingbird fell into it. Its eyes had been pecked out, its beak was missing, and I could see its heart beating through its torn chest. The heart began to fall out, so I put my finger there to hold its heart in. It felt more like a vibration than a heartbeat, like a moth's wing. It felt good on my finger. Then another broken hummingbird fell, but into the pond. It made a few ripples and then floated there on its side, left leg twitching, beak frozen open, stiff little creature with one wing straight up. A little paper sail boat. The clouds were not shaped like clouds. A tree was blooming with broken hummingbirds instead of leaves. Instead of a sun, a slow explosion. The hummingbird heart on my finger felt bottomless. The day almost smelled like spring.

DEAD HUMMINGBIRD PROBLEM

A dead hummingbird falls from a tree and then more dead hummingbirds fall from more trees. All the dead hummingbirds. All the trees. Falling from trees becomes a new kind of flight. Everything that has died becomes a dead hummingbird. The dead hummingbird becomes the new atom and the hearts of the dead hummingbird, unbeating and indivisible, become the new subatomic particles. The smell becomes an unbearable steam.

I know a place where we can escape the dead hummingbird problem, a pond no one knows about, cold and clean. It is fed by a mountain stream. We can take off all our clothes there and maybe have sex.

MORE AND MORE JAGUAR

You were becoming more and more jaguar. Your side toes hung like dew-claws. When you were hungry, you slid down the tree in which we perched, and left the woods on all four legs for the first time. You returned with blood matted in the short brittle hairs along your jawbone. I wanted to tell you how lately I've been feeling compressed, as if into a miniature cube, unable to move my limbs, unable to see clearly, but you were too animal at that point, too blood on your jawbone. This was one million years ago. Now most everything is jaguar. There's one on the tundra bursting with hundreds of beautiful pink blossoms. There's one slowly eating a hole into your lower intestine.

I WAS SURROUNDED BY A MOB OF PEOPLE

I was surrounded by a mob of people. I showed my teeth. I kicked many of them in the ribs. Many of them kicked me back, in the ribs. One of them had the face of my dead mother and one of them had the face of my dead father. One of them had my face. I asked the one with my face where he got that face, but he only echoed exactly what I asked and then, just like I did, waited impatiently for an answer. *Where did you get that face? Where did you get that face? Where did you get that face? Where did you get that face?*

This back and forth went on for a very long time, then there was a long loaded silence until I felt my skeleton arm move my arm arm up toward his mouth and my skeleton finger move my finger finger onto his lips while his arm moved toward my mouth and while his finger touched my lips. We were like babies again.

THE WORLD BECAME TOO LARGE SO IT WAS DIVIDED INTO MANY SMALLER WORLDS

The world became too large so it was divided into many smaller worlds. People, also, became too large and there was exactly one person per new world. My world was filled with thousands of giant moths. It was difficult to breath without inhaling a giant moth. My own body, then, was like an even smaller world filled with inhaled giant moths. Also, my insides were a lot like birthday cake, so the giant moths were stuck and unable to flutter around. The giant moths that I did not inhale, I tried to trap in a suitcase that I "borrowed" from a family of nomads one summer. They kept clothes and food in it, but it was perfect for trapping moths. I told them I'd bring it back with a sticker on it from some place exotic, like maybe Mexóco.

THE WORLD

It is black.
It is a giant cage.
It is the inside of the skull
of a moth
let go above the open sea.

THE BLACK HOLE

When I show someone the black hole it is difficult for me not to push that person into it. I'm not sure what that means but it frightens me. Sometimes when I go to the black hole by myself, I'm afraid I might jump into it despite my own resistance. I'm afraid of myself. It's as if I've been given someone else's heart and someone else has mine, as if our hearts had been switched while we slept. One day, when all the continents have been buried in ocean, we'll slowly float past each other in our little boats, hearing our own hearts in each other's chests, and watch each other like stars we don't know are dead.

INVISIBLE AND NOT INVISIBLE

A woman gives birth to identical twins. One is named Invisible and the other is named Not Invisible. One you can *not* see and the other you *can* see. The one you can *not* see is named Invisible. The one you *can* see is named Not Invisible. She raises both of them in a house. Though they are both always at her side and always at each other's side, she grieves for the one you can not see, Invisible. *O Invisible, O Invisible* she cries while looking at Not Invisible. After a while, it becomes difficult to tell them apart.

WHEN I FIND MY ANIMAL LIGHT, MOM, I WILL CONVINCE MYSELF IT IS BEAUTIFUL

I try to find my way home through the woods at night. There is no moon and no stars. My eyes never adjust. My hands are in front of me feeling for trees but I don't feel any. I feel like I'm walking down a hill but I can't be sure. I hear a small crowd cheering and I walk toward the cheering but the cheering never gets louder. Then the cheering turns into moths and then the moths fly away. There are no sounds at all in the world. I go back up the hill a little and then stop. I stand still in the middle of the silent world. I feel like a single celled organism, translucent and amorphous, but I know I'm not. I can feel my arms and legs on my body. Then I squat down and put my knees against my chest and put my arms around my shins and put my head between my knees.

Outside of my body is darkness and inside of my body is nothing but light. Both are blinding. I chop down a tree and build a house. The outside of the house is darkness and the inside of the house is nothing but light. I establish a parade route in a perfect circle in the darkness around the house. It is too dark to see any of the floats, but they can be heard. I can hear some clapping and laughing, a marching band playing *Nothing but the Blood* and the growl of caged jaguars. There is only one thing that can be seen: Satan. Satan is floating endlessly, tirelessly, a few feet off the ground along the parade route outside of my house, arms crossed across his fiery chest. He looks like he's made of glowing rock, cracking with the pressure of hot gaseous lava. Lava is spilling out of his hollowed eye sockets. His hair is wind-swept wild-fire. The heat that radiates from his body keeps my house very warm. Like a clock, he slowly floats past the front window of my house at noon and midnight. It is how I keep time. It is Satan's job to keep time. It is Satan's job to be the only light in the darkness. Some people think it is Satan's job to make what is wrong with this world, but those people are wrong. It is Satan's job to make us choose between the only two things that are right with it.

YOU MUST CHOOSE BETWEEN FLOATING ETERNALLY IN A BUOYANT CAGE OF HUMMINGBIRD BONES DOWN A RIVER OF LAVA OR A RIVER OF BLOOD

You must choose
between floating
eternally in a buoyant cage
of hummingbird bones
down a river of lava
or a river of   blood.

Hmm. River
of lava or
river of   blood.

Lava or   blood.

I'd choose the river
of   blood.

I'd float eternally
in a buoyant cage
of hummingbird bones
down a river of   blood.

A HORRIBLE FLOOD OF LAVA

A horrible flood of lava moves quickly into town. The pots in my kitchen begin to rattle. I climb onto the roof and find the horrible flood of lava through my rooftop telescope. When the horrible flood of lava gets close enough, I see it is not lava at all, but a horrible mob of hooded men burning the black night with fiery torches, demanding my head. I wave a fiery torch back at them to scare them off, to demonstrate that I will not surrender easily. They yell in a strange and angry language. It sounds a little like this:

Na na na na kya kya kya.
Na na na na kya kya kya.
Na na na na kya kya kya.
Na na na na kya kya kya.

When the mob gets even closer I can see through my rooftop telescope that it is not actually a mob, but the woods on fire. And not the woods on fire but my fingers. And not my fingers but someone else's finger pressing unmercifully against the back of my eyeball.

GOODBYE LESSON

I have to say goodbye. I've been adopted. I'll grow up in the house on the hill with all the bats. One of my parents will be part-night, part-tree. The other will be part-person, part-insect. My new sister will be part-night, part-tree, part-person, part-insect. They will all eventually die in a farm accident/wolf-mauling. I am part-wolf, part-farm accident. I will be cursed with a life without end, eternally trekking through the woods in a time when the woods cover ¾ of the world. I will meet many new people and these people will be mostly all-person. You will be an exception: part-hummingbird, part-caterpillar. I will watch you eat yourself to death. When you push your own last foot through your own beak, I will miss you dearly, and again I will miss you when your beak is swallowed. At that point, I will know that goodbyes are when you eat yourself to death.

SIN AND FORGIVENESS

When my mouth opens to ask for forgiveness a little girl crawls out. She crawls into a house in the woods and grows up in its warm yellow light. The house has dark floral wallpaper and a fireplace. Half of all of the people in the world crawl out of my mouth when I open it to ask for forgiveness. The other half of all of the people in the world crawl out of my mouth when I sin. Half of the people are born from forgiveness and half are born from sin. This creates a perfect balance, a perfect world. Balance is very important. The Water Cycle is another example.

THE FIRE CYCLE

There are trees and they are on fire. There are hummingbirds and they are on fire. There are graves and they are on fire and the things coming out of the graves are on fire. The house you grew up in is on fire. There is a gigantic trebuchet on fire on the edge of a crater and the crater is on fire. There is a complex system of tunnels deep underneath the surface with only one entrance and one exit and the entire system is filled with fire. There is a wooden cage we're trapped in, too large to see, and it is on fire. There are jaguars on fire. Wolves. Spiders. Wolf-spiders on fire. If there were people. If our fathers were alive. If we had a daughter. Fire to the edges. Fire in the river beds. Fire between the mattresses of the bed you were born in. Fire in your mother's belly. There is a little boy wearing a fire shirt holding a baby lamb. There is a little girl in a fire skirt asking if she can ride the baby lamb like a horse. There is you on top of me with thighs of fire while a hot red fog hovers in your hair. There is me on top of you wearing a fire shirt and then pulling the fire shirt over my head and tossing it like a fireball through the fog at a new kind of dinosaur. There are meteorites disintegrating in the atmosphere just a few thousand feet above us and tiny fireballs are falling down around us, pooling around us, forming a kind of fire lake which then forms a kind of fire cloud. There is this feeling I get when I am with you. There is our future house burning like a star on the hill. There is our dark flickering shadow. There is my hand on fire in your hand on fire, my body on fire above your body on fire, our tongues made of ash. We are rocks on a distant and uninhabitable planet. We have our whole life ahead of us.

LOVE IS WHEN A BOAT IS BUILT
FROM ALL THE EYELASHES IN THE OCEAN

When the bats
break
from the mouth of
the cave
hold on tight
at my waist.

If I fall
into the ocean
bury what washes up
beneath the mattress
of my first bed.

When our eyelashes fall out
it does not mean we are about to die
it means we are about to be saved.

We should look
directly into the sun.

We should
expect a boat.

THE HISTORIES

The Chair Age

I set a table for one.
There is no table.
I spread a sheet across it.
I place the dishes.
There is no sheet.
There are no dishes.
When I sit in a chair
I am sitting
in a chair.

The Dishes Age

A chair rots beneath me.
There is no chair.
I carve a set of dishes.
I set the table.
There is no table.
The dishes crash to the floor
at my feet.
There is no floor.

The Table Age

I make a chandelier
out of broken dishes.
There is no chandelier.
There are no dishes.
I stand on the table
to hang the chandelier
from the ceiling.
The chandelier reflects light
onto the floor.
There is no ceiling.
There is no light.
There is no floor.
The table moves like
it is moving
but it is not moving.

The Floor Age

The chandelier crashes.
There is no chandelier.

The Chandelier Age

I sit in a chair.
There is no chair.

The Sheet Age

I place a sheet on the table.
There is no table.
A sheet floats slowly down
to the broken dishes.
There are no dishes
but the sheet is shaped
like dishes.

The Ghost Age

A sheet is hanging
from the chandelier.
There are two tiny eye-holes
in the sheet.
There is no sheet.
There is no chandelier.

THE POND

I am born in a boat with one paddle.
The sky is full of holes from which fog comes out.
The swans are so still I think they are part of my eyeballs.
I rub my eyeballs with my fists.
I have two eyeballs.
I have two fists.
I make a list of everything I have on my head
and then cross it all out.
I have a complete skeletal system
with skin all over it.
Little blind thing,
it's what you see when you look at me.

A thing in the pond at night
looks a little like a face
and has a gravitational pull.
I am 9 months old in a boat tied to a string
floating toward the thing
that looks like a face.
Now I am a year in a crib
tree limbs bendy in the window.
Now I am a year and 3 months in an open field when I learn:
if there is a shadow of a tree and no trees around
I am the tree.

I invented a language that isn't little bird calls.
I can fit a number of things in my pants.
I invented a time machine.
It tells you what time it is.
I invented a love machine.
It tells you it loves you.
I invented the vibrating bed
and how it makes you feel.
I invented the way leaves hide a pond.
My whole life I imagine
a man-eating jaguar
hungry on the horizon.

I am a boy who lives in the woods.
I fall in love with trees, mostly.
When I touch them
they turn to wood.
When I touch you
you turn into a pond.
I walk into a pond
like I love it.

I am sleeping on a chair with very long legs
in the middle of a pond.
I don't have a name.
You don't know what to call me.
You try making animal noises
but I'm sleeping
so I can't hear you.
Then you start to sleep.
Now everyone is sleeping at the same time.
You don't have a name either.
Sleeping is a place where there are no names.

I ride a horse out of a town
and into the pond.
We are still for a while, the horse and I.
The swans swim in one big circle around us.
I have a habit of leaving a place
I don't know how to get back to.
I have a habit of leaving the place.
Don't hate me for what I have become.
I am sorry I missed your birthday party I say
but I say it like a horse.

My legs fit perfectly in my pants.
My leg bones fit so perfectly in my legs.
I'm in a little boat making circles on the pond.
Jaguars are on the horizon
eating, eating.

It is difficult to tell what will happen next.
Maybe we'll hold hands
and walk down to the pond.
Maybe a bat will fly into the pond
and swim around
like it's having fun
but then it'll struggle and start to die.
We'll watch it start to die.
We'll agree that we understand how the bat feels.
We'll say *I know the feeling*
but we won't know the feeling.
The feeling we'll know
is more like being on a chair
with really long legs
sinking slowly into the pond
on a beautiful day.

I find an abandoned hotel
with 1000 replicas of my first bed
each giving off a faint golden light.
I pretend to sleep in each one.
This takes one year.
One night, I hear someone say *hey wake up*.
I have no idea who it could be
so I keep pretending to sleep.
I keep pretending to dream
about hummingbirds in the bathtub
a bat in the pond
a brother I've never seen trapped in the basement
a bear with no legs
a barge tied on a kite string.

There is a bear with no legs
growling at the edge of the pond.
There is a lot of blood
where its legs used to be.
It grows tired of growling
and quietly stares at me.
We sat there for a while
just looking at each other.
How do I save you, Bear?
I thought very hard
and eventually got behind it
then pushed it like a gigantic baby
into the pond.

I hover above the pond
like a ghost hovering
above the wrong funeral.
I watch a person who looks like me swimming around.
I plan to watch him forever.
This is some kind of bravery.

I begin a new life as someone else.
I am a baby at first
then I grow to be very old
and when I die
there is no one to bury me.
It is foggy and quiet.
A pushed-over tree.
Black birds hanging from strings.
A pond with swans and dead horses in it.
A beeping sound.

If I could invent a town
I'd invent a town on a pond
with boats scattered everywhere
in a dark fog.
When you come to town
I'll be sleeping in one of the boats
but you'll find me right away.
It'll be quiet.
We'll be hungry so we'll eat some bananas
then we'll push off
past the outskirts of town
past the last empty boat.
I'll show you the cave
where all the bats come from.
You'll show me that place
between your knees
where my hand goes.

At the edge of the pond
someone who looks like me
is holding hands
with someone who looks like you.
I begin to wonder who I am
because I don't look like me.

Leaves spill onto the pond
until it disappears.
It looks like a leaf-covered field.
My body is designed
for more than one thing.
I am inside myself, fogging myself up.

I am tired but my bed is nowhere.
I've been walking in one large circle my entire life
past piles of things.
A pile of old time machines.
A pile of horses.
A pond with bikes and kites in it.
An old parade unhinging on the horizon.

I have never seen the place
where the parade ends
where it just *ends*
so you promise to show me the place
where the parade just ends
and when we get there
there is a pond with swans.
You want to sleep on the rocks.
I knew this would happen.
I wish we were more French.
You have regular eyes.
A big holiday feels just around the corner.

Everything above the pond is alive
and everything below the pond is not alive.
I am a reflection of myself
looking at myself.

I found a dead body in the pond.
I arranged a funeral for it
but nobody showed up.
Turns out, it didn't belong to anyone.
Turns out, it was the wrong
kind of body for a funeral.
I feel like I'm hovering
just above myself
but it turns out we both are.

I rise up out of the pond
and put on a pair of pants
then outgrow the pants.
I'm shown my place at a table.
My whole life is a ripping sound.
I try to be brave.

You spend most of the day in the pond.
Every time you blink your eyelashes fall out
and then quickly grow back.
I spend all day collecting them.
They're what I make boats out of.
We like to ride bikes and fly kites together.

I haven't done everything I've wanted.
I haven't made one of those Viking ships
with a dragon on the bow.
I haven't raided Europe.
I'm just going to sit here on this pond
and make some holes in this boat
for your arms to come up through.

The world ends for a long time.
The pond is frozen.
My boat is half-buried in the ice.
Dead birds are lined up on the horizon.
Dead jaguars are stiff at the pond edge,
claws gripping the ice.
A dead body that looks like me
is propped up in a chair.
Horse ribs and bike tires.
A kite in a tree.
A bear stuck in a machine.
The parade is silent and sinking.
The world is unhinged.
You'd think I'd be scared
but I'm not scared.

INDEX